J. H. Shapiro

Magic Trash

A Story of Tyree Guyton
and His Art

Illustrated by
Vanessa Brantley-Newton

Charlesbridge

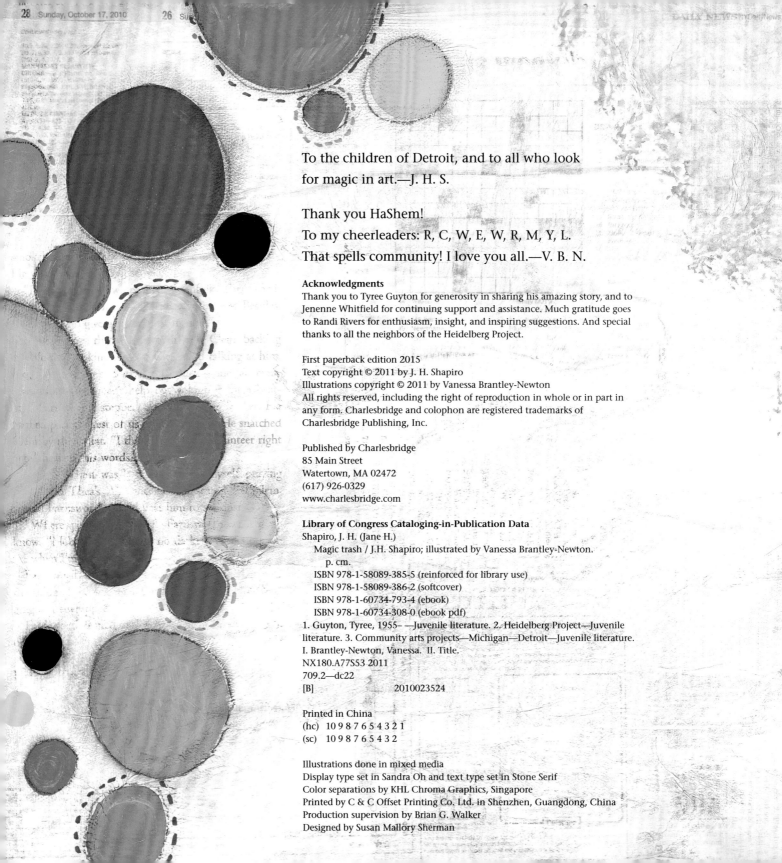

To the children of Detroit, and to all who look
for magic in art.—J. H. S.

Thank you HaShem!
To my cheerleaders: R, C, W, E, W, R, M, Y, L.
That spells community! I love you all.—V. B. N.

Acknowledgments
Thank you to Tyree Guyton for generosity in sharing his amazing story, and to
Jenenne Whitfield for continuing support and assistance. Much gratitude goes
to Randi Rivers for enthusiasm, insight, and inspiring suggestions. And special
thanks to all the neighbors of the Heidelberg Project.

First paperback edition 2015
Text copyright © 2011 by J. H. Shapiro
Illustrations copyright © 2011 by Vanessa Brantley-Newton

Published by Charlesbridge
85 Main Street
Watertown, MA 02472
(617) 926-0329
www.charlesbridge.com

Library of Congress Cataloging-in-Publication Data
Shapiro, J. H. (Jane H.)
   Magic trash / J.H. Shapiro; illustrated by Vanessa Brantley-Newton.
      p. cm.
   ISBN 978-1-58089-385-5 (reinforced for library use)
   ISBN 978-1-58089-386-2 (softcover)
   ISBN 978-1-60734-793-4 (ebook)
   ISBN 978-1-60734-308-0 (ebook pdf)
1. Guyton, Tyree, 1955– —Juvenile literature. 2. Heidelberg Project—Juvenile
literature. 3. Community arts projects—Michigan—Detroit—Juvenile literature.
I. Brantley-Newton, Vanessa. II. Title.
NX180.A77S53 2011
709.2—dc22
[B]   2010023524

Printed in China
(hc) 10 9 8 7 6 5 4 3 2 1
(sc) 10 9 8 7 6 5 4 3 2

Illustrations done in mixed media
Display type set in Sandra Oh and text type set in Stone Serif
Color separations by KHL Chroma Graphics, Singapore
Printed by C & C Offset Printing Co. Ltd. in Shenzhen, Guangdong, China
Production supervision by Brian G. Walker
Designed by Susan Mallory Sherman

A winter chill whooshed down Heidelberg Street. Young Tyree Guyton buttoned his coat—*pop!* His last button flipped into the gutter. He dove after it, then dug through frosty leaves. He pried a Popsicle stick from the ice. He hoisted a bicycle wheel off the curb. He scooped up a baseball cap buried in the snow.

Pockets clanking, Tyree darted home—a home on the East Side of Detroit that already bulged with ten children.

"Shop around," Tyree sang along with the radio as he unloaded the day's finds. His mama didn't earn enough money sewing and cleaning to buy new shoes, much less bikes and balls. So he zapped fun into amazing junk that others tossed away.

Popsicle sticks became boards to build a house. The cap soared like a rocket ship.

The wheel bounced, spokes jumping. Dots danced.

Let rockets fly!

Boards tower high.

Bounce, jump, and dance, magic trash!

Tyree barely heard the *thump-thwack* of his brothers' games while
he dreamed up designs. In school he sat alone, drawing pictures.
When his report card arrived, his aunt asked, "Is Tyree dumb?"
"Maybe crazy?" his mama whispered.

Then one sunny day when Tyree was nine, his grandpa Sam, a house painter, plopped a brush into his hands. "Paint the world," Grandpa said.

Tyree dipped into Grandpa's cans of color, sloshing purple, slapping yellow, aiming his brush like a magic wand. Abracadabra! Tyree's shyness vanished.

Sweet apples crunched when he glopped the red. He'd never seen Lake Huron, but now it splashed in a pool of blue.

"Like new," Grandpa said of a glistening ladder. Tyree smiled and swirled a shade of green.

Other kids on his street giggled and razzed:
"Look at his green face. Ha! Green junk."

Still, as Tyree zoomed from
bent bottle caps to rusty
wheels, Grandpa Sam's words
twirled in his head.

"I'm going to be an artist," Tyree said.

His mama hung her head. "That's not a job."

He peered into Grandpa's twinkling eyes.

Tyree clenched his brush. He would be an artist . . . *yes*.

Brush greens and blues
On wheels and shoes.
Slosh, slap, and splash magic trash.

At age twelve Tyree squinted into spiraling smoke as National Guard tanks rolled down nearby Mt. Elliott Street. All his life, neighbors had raced out of town to live in new suburbs. Now some who had stayed exploded in rage, like shaken bottles of Vernors ginger ale. Tyree gawked, teeth chattering. Rioters were burning buildings in *his* neighborhood.

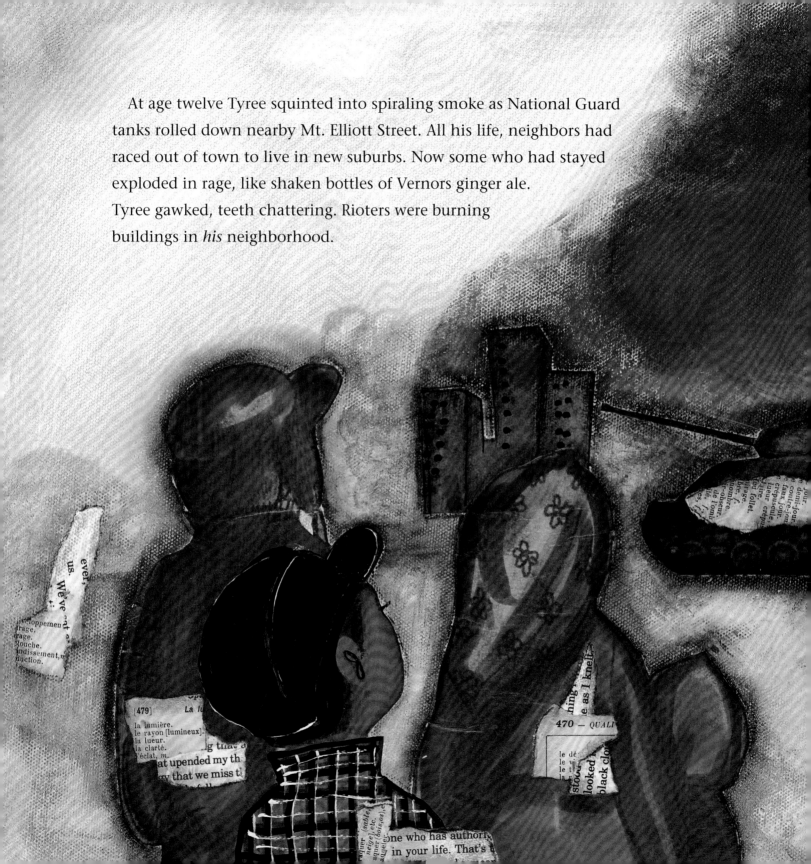

When he grew to be sixteen, Tyree, too, left the shapes and hues
of Heidelberg Street to seek a new life.

He marched as a soldier.

He inspected cars in a factory.

He doused fires as a firefighter.

HEIDELBERG

But he never forgot about painting his world, so he enrolled
in art school to learn more about colors, lines, and designs.
At last Tyree bolted back home to Heidelberg.

When he returned, though, his street had changed. Houses
sat deserted, creeping with spirits of owners who had run away
from the neighborhood. Tyree tripped over trash, lots of trash.

And troublemakers lurked. They snuck into hollow houses;
they even set fire to one.

Whoo! Spirits whirl.

New troubles swirl.

Kick, burn, and hurl magic trash.

"No," cried Tyree, "not on this street!"
His mama still lived in the same home.
Grandpa Sam painted pictures, inside now.

Tyree grabbed his brush and burrowed through rubbish.
He cast spells on suitcases, toilets, and a slide trombone.
   Before the colors dried, Grandpa Sam hurried out to help.
   They painted a busted bus. They tied shoes to trees.
They flung broken bikes and cast-off tires on burned-out
buildings and forgotten yards. And they painted *Faces of God*
in blue, black, and orange.

Their street sparkled.

When trouble still sizzled in one discarded home, Tyree coated it in dots and squares of pink, blue, yellow, and purple, then perched a magenta watchdog on the porch . . . dopey dealing thieves hustled from its view, chased away by bright paint and barking trash.

Tyree named one home *Dotty Wotty* and another *Fun House.* Spying hungry, crying children, he dangled broken baby dolls on telephone poles and rooftops. Dolls sobbed with each puff of wind. Maybe now others would see.

Bright colors flash.

Scared dealers dash.

Bark, cry, and swing, magic trash.

Some people squawked about garbage. A few neighbors complained to the city.

The mayor and his helpers stomped.

Soon bulldozers roared up to the project to crush every doll and board.

"You can't do that!" yelled neighbors as dust swooped to the treetops.

"Get out of here!" others screamed. "Tyree's trash is beautiful."

Tyree scrambled to snatch a few pieces. "This is my art," he cried. But the dots and stripes and baby dolls lay bashed and smashed and still.

Tyree rubbed his eyes. Grandpa Sam poked at piles.

Old houses talk.

Some neighbors squawk.

Crash, bash, and smash magic trash.

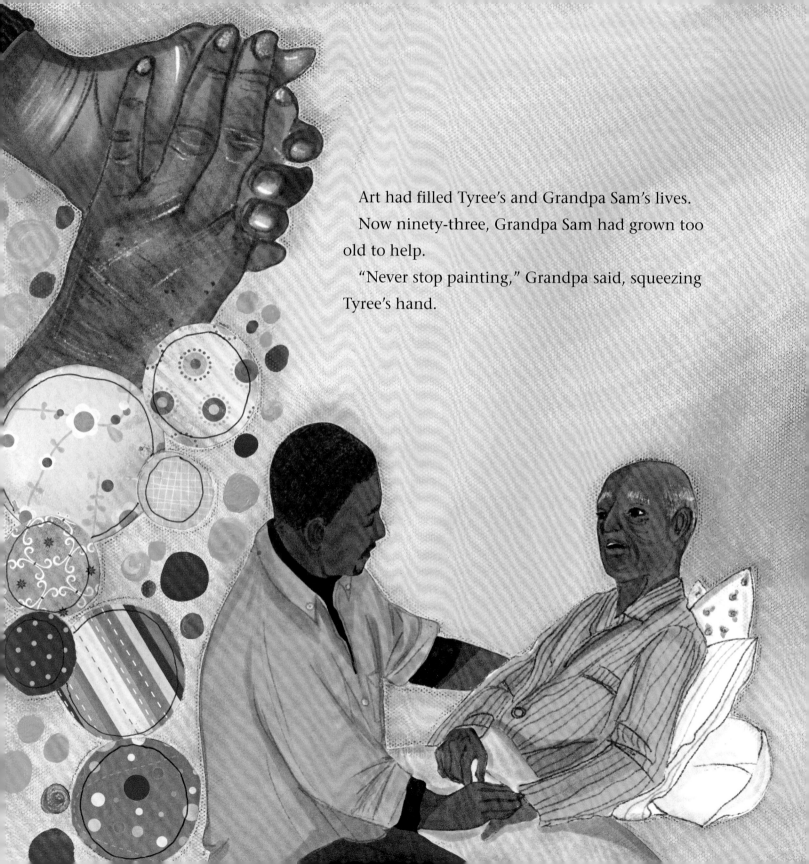

Art had filled Tyree's and Grandpa Sam's lives.
Now ninety-three, Grandpa Sam had grown too old to help.

"Never stop painting," Grandpa said, squeezing Tyree's hand.

And then Tyree stood alone with brushes, paint, and trash.

He wasn't alone for long, though.

"We can help," neighbors called.

"Your colors and dots chased away those thieves."

Together they shoveled, swept, and hauled in new trash.

Then after eight years of painting and rebuilding,
neighbors heard wreckers *screech* a second time. *Faces of God* watched
while the city crushed two more houses.

"No-o-o!" Tyree yelled.

Tyree and his neighbors were hopping mad.

"This street is ours," they said.

"We'll never quit!"

They marched downtown to tell their story
to a judge and jury.

The city argued that Heidelberg Street
was a garbage dump.

NO, decided the court. *It is art!*

Tyree's work survived.

The next day Tyree and his neighbors began anew, aiming their brushes like magic wands. Children sang as they hammererd and spattered designs. Even former troublemakers returned, ready to rake, sweep, and build. United by trash, they cast a spell on the street, brightening their home for good.

Word of Heidelberg Street spread far; it blazed across the air. Folks from Canada, Kenya, and Japan scurried to the neighborhood. They stared: "Wow, look at that!"

Tyree waved his brush. "Welcome."

In a warm breeze, dots danced, gleaming castoffs jangled and jumped.

Let rockets fly!

Boards tower high.

Author's Note

Magic Trash is based on the life and art of painter and sculptor Tyree Guyton (b. 1955).

In 2011 the Heidelberg Project celebrated its twenty-fifth anniversary. Tyree continues to work on Heidelberg Street and travels internationally to lecture and assist with installations of community art. He represented the United States in the 2008 Venice Architecture Biennale.

You may visit the Heidelberg Project in Detroit or view Tyree Guyton's art in museums, including the Detroit Institute of Arts. Discover more about his work at www.heidelberg.org.

Bibliography

Heidelberg Project. *Connecting the Dots: Tyree Guyton's Heidelberg Project.* Detroit: Wayne State University Press, 2007.

Come Unto Me: The Faces of Tyree Guyton. DVD. Directed by Nicole Cattell. New York: Naked Eye Productions, 1999.

Photos: (left) Tyree Guyton painting the Mt. Elliott House, courtesy of the Heidelberg Project Archives; (right) *New White House,* courtesy of Michelle Figurski. Used with permission.